DEALING WITH
MENTAL DISORDERS

DEALING WITH

GENDER DYSPHORIA

By Martha Lundin

ReferencePoint
Press®

San Diego, CA

For more information, contact:
ReferencePoint Press, Inc.
PO Box 27779
San Diego, CA 92198
www.ReferencePointPress.com

Content Consultant: Carla Marie Manly, PhD

LIBRARY OF CONGRESS CATALOGING-IN-PUBLICATION DATA

Names: Lundin, Martha, 1993– author.
Title: Dealing with gender dysphoria / Martha Lundin.
Description: San Diego : ReferencePoint Press, [2020] | Series: Dealing with mental disorders | Includes bibliographical references and index. | Audience: Grades 10-12
Identifiers: LCCN 2019034016 (print) | LCCN 2019034017 (eBook) | ISBN 9781682827918 (hardcover) | ISBN 9781682827925 (eBook)
Subjects: LCSH: Gender identity disorders--Juvenile literature.
Classification: LCC RC560.G45 L86 2020 (print) | LCC RC560.G45 (ebook) | DDC 616.85/83--dc23
C record available at https://lccn.loc.gov/2019034016
ebook record available at https://lccn.loc.gov/2019034017

CONTENTS

AIDEN'S STORY

Aiden is transgender. When he was born, the doctors told his parents he was a girl. They raised him as if he were a girl, but Aiden hasn't ever been comfortable in his own skin. He's in high school now, but when he was little, he only wanted to play with toys typically associated with boys. Aiden shaved off all of his dolls' hair so they could have short hair.

Growing up, Aiden didn't understand why he had to wear a different swimsuit than his friends who were boys. Aiden hated when his mom put him in dresses. And when his relatives called him "little lady," it felt like there were bugs crawling under his skin.

Last year, when Aiden was in eighth grade, he told his parents he was transgender. When Aiden started going through puberty, all the discomfort he felt as a little kid got worse. His body was changing in ways he didn't like. His hips were growing wider and his chest was getting bigger. Aiden didn't want either of those things to happen.

He started having panic attacks during gym class. The only way he could change into his gym clothes was if he went into a bathroom stall. Girls in Aiden's class whispered that they thought he was weird.

People with gender dysphoria struggle to feel comfortable in their own skin. Having a support group can help.

Aiden didn't have anyone to talk to except his closest friend, Alex. Aiden started skipping school. If he wasn't in school, his teachers couldn't call him by the wrong name and pronouns. Then he wouldn't have to deal with a racing pulse and sweaty palms. His classmates wouldn't laugh at him because they thought he was dressed in the wrong clothes.

When Aiden told his parents he was trans, they were very accepting. They were good at listening. Aiden told them about skipping school. He also told them about his anxiety and his loneliness. His parents helped him, and they sought help for themselves, too.

Aiden saw a pediatrician with his parents over the summer. She told Aiden he was experiencing something called gender dysphoria (GD).

Therapy is an important part of managing gender dysphoria. Therapists can help people with gender dysphoria find treatment options.

GD is the distress that some people experience when their expressed gender is different from their assigned gender. Going to a knowledgeable and supportive doctor really helped Aiden and his family. The doctor suggested that Aiden begin socially transitioning. He could use a boy's name and wear boys' clothes that made him feel confident. But she also told him it was important to find a good therapist to talk to.

When they got home, Aiden and his parents wrote a letter to the teachers at the high school where Aiden would be starting in the fall. The letter explained that Aiden was no longer going by the name he was given at birth and that he was using masculine pronouns now. The letter made sure teachers were aware of Aiden's identity before school started.

A lot of things have gotten better for Aiden. Some days are still hard. People started calling him by his name and pronouns at school. This helped lessen his anxiety. But many of Aiden's classmates knew him before he started transitioning. Some of them mess up his pronouns or call him by his old name. Most of the time it's an accident, but some of his other classmates make fun of him for his high voice. Those are the days when his dysphoria makes it hard for Aiden to go to school.

Aiden wants his appearance to match his identity. Hormone therapy can help. Testosterone would make his voice lower, and he'd grow facial hair. His parents told him he could start hormone therapy over the summer. For now, Aiden is on a medication to help him with his anxiety, and he sees a therapist once a week. He is still working on good coping mechanisms when his dysphoria is bad. With time, Aiden knows he'll be able to manage his gender dysphoria.

TERMS AND TOPICS

Gender dysphoria affects a lot of people. This disorder is most often experienced by people in the transgender community. Discussions of gender dysphoria include some terms that readers may not be familiar with. These terms include *transgender* (trans), *cisgender* (cis), *gender nonconforming* (GNC), and *gender variant*. These terms describe different gender expressions and identities. Gender is not the same as sex. Sex is a medical term that is most often used to describe the reproductive organs of a person.

It is important to understand that gender identity is not the same as sexual orientation. Sexual orientation describes whom a person is attracted to. Gender identity is how a person sees themselves—as a boy, a girl, or neither. There are many different gender identities. Some people may want to transition to their true gender. People who transition may identify as transgender. A transgender person is someone who was assigned a different sex at birth than their gender identity.

GLAAD is an organization that works to create more inclusive media for lesbian, gay, bisexual, transgender, and queer people (LGBTQ). When founded, GLAAD stood for Gay and Lesbian Alliance Against Defamation. In order to be more inclusive, it is now known simply as GLAAD. GLAAD explains transition as a process that goes beyond surgeries. It says: "Transition is the accurate term that does not fixate on surgeries, which many transgender people do not or cannot undergo. Terms like 'pre-op' or 'post-op' unnecessarily fixate on a person's anatomy and should be avoided."[1] Some transgender people choose to change their body to fit their identity. Others choose not to. Transitioning is a complex process that is different for every person.

Studies on gender dysphoria are limited. Approximately .005 percent to .014 percent of people assigned male at birth are diagnosed with gender dysphoria. The figure for those assigned female at birth is .002 percent to .003 percent. However, these figures likely underestimate the true numbers, as they are based only on people who seek formal treatment.

> "Transition is the accurate term that does not fixate on surgeries."[1]
>
> – GLAAD

Gender dysphoria is complicated, and sometimes dysphoria can look like other mental illnesses such as anxiety and depression. It can affect every aspect of a person's life, and it can be even more disruptive when it affects adolescents. Getting treatment for gender dysphoria, along with help from a broad support network, can help people with GD feel more confident in their bodies and gender identities.

UNDERSTANDING
GENDER AND
SEXUALITY

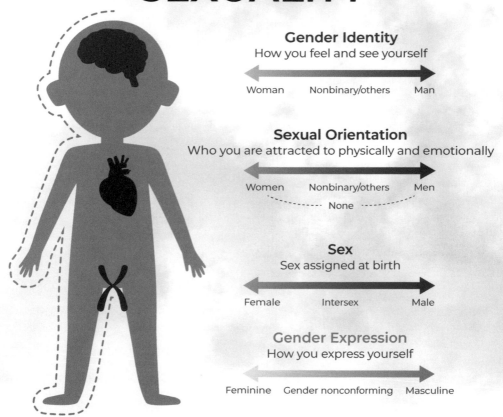

Gender Identity
How you feel and see yourself

Woman   Nonbinary/others   Man

Sexual Orientation
Who you are attracted to physically and emotionally

Women   Nonbinary/others   Men

None

Sex
Sex assigned at birth

Female   Intersex   Male

Gender Expression
How you express yourself

Feminine   Gender nonconforming   Masculine

This graphic explains some of the terms and concepts explored in this book related to sex, sexual orientation, and gender identity.

CHAPTER
ONE

WHAT IS
GENDER
DYSPHORIA?

G ender dysphoria is a mental disorder. It is a condition that causes a person to experience anxiety and significant distress because their assigned gender does not match their gender identity. People with gender dysphoria face significant challenges. Some of them are societal, such as bullying or discrimination. Others stem from internalized prejudices, such as a fear of disappointing others. Transgender populations are most at risk for a diagnosis of gender dysphoria. Transgender people face barriers to health care and employment and are more likely to be the victim of a hate crime.

Gender dysphoria has a high co-occurrence with other mental disorders such as depression and anxiety. These disorders need to be treated in conjunction with gender dysphoria. In general, treating only gender dysphoria will not cure the other disorders. Similarly, treating only the co-occurring disorders will not entirely solve the distress that gender dysphoria causes.

Transgender people are the most likely to be diagnosed with gender dysphoria. They face challenges such as discrimination and fear of disappointing others.

A person's assigned sex and their gender identity are not always different. But for people with gender dysphoria, a mismatch between them causes distress. Many people think sex and gender are the same, but they are different. Sex describes the various biological male and female factors that include sex hormones, gonads, and certain internal and external genitalia of a person. Gender is the way a person feels about their body. Sometimes sex and gender identity match. But they don't always. Some people also believe that sex and gender are a binary. A binary is a two-option system: male or female, and boy or girl. However, scientific studies show that both are much more complex. This complex is causing many people to call for a change in the way society talks about sex and gender in order to be more inclusive of all biological and social identities.

ASSIGNED SEX

When a baby is born, doctors look at the baby's genitals to determine if it is male or female. This is the baby's assigned sex. Many people differentiate sex and gender by defining sex as a series of biological indicators. In contrast, gender is a social identity.

But even this definition is too simple. In her book *Bodies in Doubt*, Elizabeth Reis writes, "In the United States and most other places, humans are men or they are women; they may not be neither or both. Yet not all bodies are clearly male or female."[2] Some people are born intersex.

ENDING GENITAL SURGERIES FOR INTERSEX CHILDREN

Intersex advocates are working to ban the genital surgeries that are often performed on children with ambiguous genitalia. There are many reasons that advocates are working toward this goal. Activists call the surgeries genital mutilation. There is nothing medically necessary about performing the surgeries on the infants. The children are too young to give consent to the surgeries. There have even been cases where the doctors perform the surgeries without fully explaining them to parents.

Doctors who defend the practice of genital surgeries say that reconstructing sex organs is necessary to give the child a normal childhood. However, definitions about what is a normal childhood are based on societal norms. This does not take into account typical gender and sexual variance. These surgeries are performed throughout the person's childhood, up to about puberty. However, during puberty, some intersex children find that they do not identify with their assigned gender. This can sometimes lead to gender dysphoria and more reconstructive surgeries later in adolescence and early adulthood. Advocates urge lawmakers to pass laws that ban genital surgeries on intersex children until the children are old enough to give informed consent to the surgery.

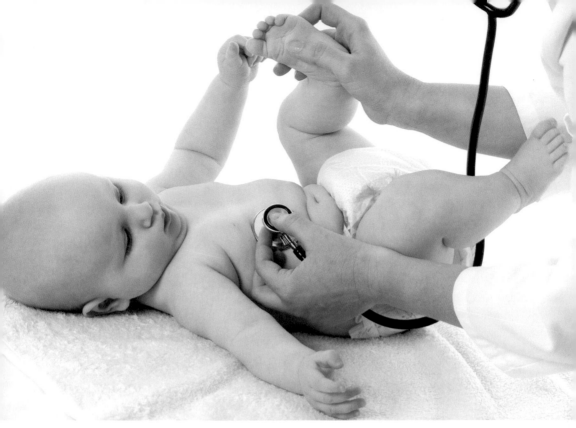

Doctors assign a baby's sex at birth. This is made complicated when babies are born intersex.

Intersex people may have an extra X or Y chromosome, or they may be missing a chromosome. Chromosomes are the genetic code that determines a person's appearance and other characteristics. People with XX chromosomes are considered female. XY people are considered male. Intersex people might also have ambiguous genitalia. Without complete genetic testing, intersex population estimates are hard to create. However, experts in the field say that approximately 1 in 1,000 infants is born intersex.

For infants with ambiguous genitalia, it is difficult for the doctor to label them as either male or female. Doctors often perform medically unnecessary, cosmetic surgeries on intersex children. Surgeon and author Dr. I.W. Gregorio said:

I think that there is a bias among medical professionals to 'fix' intersex, based on a lot of assumptions that doctors make about the 'right' ways to have sex and how a 'real' girl or boy should look. A lot of the time, surgeons are driven to operate by parents who are overwhelmed and fearful, and that it's impossible for any parent to know what their child would like in that situation.[3]

The United Nations released a statement in 2016 that said infant genital surgery could "lead to severe and life-long physical and mental pain and suffering and can amount to torture and ill-treatment."[4]

Most medical professionals agree that biological sex exists on a spectrum in the same way as gender. John Achermann studies sex development and endocrinology (the study of hormones and their role in the development of the body) at University College London's Institute of Child Health. He said, "I think there's much greater diversity within male or female, and there is certainly an area of overlap where some people can't easily define themselves within the binary structure."[5] Eric Vilain, another researcher, echoed Achermann's view of assigned sex: "Biologically, it's a spectrum."[6] Sex and gender are not the same. But one is not necessarily more concrete than the other.

> "I think there's much greater diversity within male or female, and . . . some people can't easily define themselves within the binary structure."[5]
>
> – Endocrinologist John Achermann

GENDER IDENTITY

Gender identity is how a person understands their personal gender. Many people are cisgender. This means their gender identity is the same as their assigned sex. But other people feel that their assigned sex and gender identity are different. These people may identify as transgender or nonbinary. Nonbinary people do not identify as either a boy or a girl. Gender expression is the way people dress and act according to their gender identity. People who have a gender expression that is different from stereotypical gender roles are called gender nonconforming (GNC). Gender dysphoria and GNC are different. GNC individuals may be "tomboys" or "girly" males. However, a gender nonconforming person does not suffer from the distress that dysphoria creates.

When someone's assigned sex and gender identity don't match, they can feel extremely uncomfortable. This discomfort can come from several sources. One of these is societal expectations of their assigned sex. People who have gender dysphoria may be misgendered by strangers, coworkers, and even friends and family.

A 2014 study asked transgender and nonbinary people to answer questions about being misgendered. Nearly 33 percent of respondents reported feeling stigmatized when they were misgendered. One respondent wrote:

Where I'm at school now there are way less trans and nonbinary folks, no visible trans community, and while our equity training included a video on pronouns, none of my professors or colleagues have ever asked what my pronouns are. When someone misgenders me at school I just get this shock of painful tension throughout my body.[7]

Being misgendered can make a person's gender dysphoria worse. But using a person's correct name and pronoun can ease symptoms. Nonbinary writer KC Clements explained, "It often feels difficult to ask people to use the correct pronouns for me, especially since I use they/them/theirs. People tend to push back or struggle to make the adjustment. But, when people get it right, I feel really affirmed in my nonbinary identity. I feel seen."[8]

The continued stress a person experiences when they feel like they have the wrong body can cause significant anxiety and distress. These are some of the signs of gender dysphoria. But the causes of the disorder are unclear. Symptoms of GD can occur very early in childhood. Some children exhibit signs of dysphoria as early as two years old. Other children develop dysphoria later on, often during puberty. This is when secondary sex characteristics begin to develop. Primary sex characteristics are the sexual organs. They are present from birth. Secondary sex characteristics are the outward physical signs of maturation that develop at puberty. These include growing breasts, a deepening voice, or different fat distribution.

Megan, a nonbinary person who uses she/her/hers, said it wasn't until puberty that she realized she felt differently about her body. She said:

Before I hit puberty, everything was fine. I could dress more masculine and people would accept that and say, "Oh, she's just a tomboy." I knew back then I was different. I was beginning to grow breasts, I hated them. They were always in the way of the type of clothes I liked to wear.[9]

SEARCHING FOR A CAUSE

There are hypotheses in the medical community surrounding the cause of GD. Dr. Steve Rosenthal is a professor of pediatrics who studies endocrinology. Dr. Rosenthal explained that studies show biological factors like hormones and other chemicals in the brain play a significant role in determining gender identity. He said:

> Compelling data now suggest that gender identity is not simply a psychosexual construct, but that it is influenced by biology, environmental, and cultural factors. The data that support a role of biology in gender identity development basically come from three different biomedical disciplines: from genetics, endocrinology, and brain studies.[10]

For example, researchers believe people are more likely to experience GD when there is an excess of hormones in the mother's womb during pregnancy. During development, fetuses are affected by hormones that

WHAT IS NONBINARY GENDER?

The concept of gender in much of the Western world is divided into two categories: male and female. This division is called the binary. This binary shapes almost every aspect of people's lives, from what clothes people wear, to how they style their hair, to how they deal with their emotions. While men are seen as tough and unfeeling, women are seen as soft and delicate. The binary is such a big part of society that many parents choose to have gender-reveal parties for their unborn children.

Nonbinary gender describes a range of gender identities that fall outside of the male-female binary. These identities, such as genderqueer, two-spirit, gender fluid, agender (no gender), and bigender, are often grouped under an umbrella label like "trans." Nonbinary people may choose pronouns that reflect their gender identity. Singular-they and ze/hir are two examples of gender-neutral pronouns. It is important to note, though, that not all nonbinary people use or want to use gender-neutral pronouns.

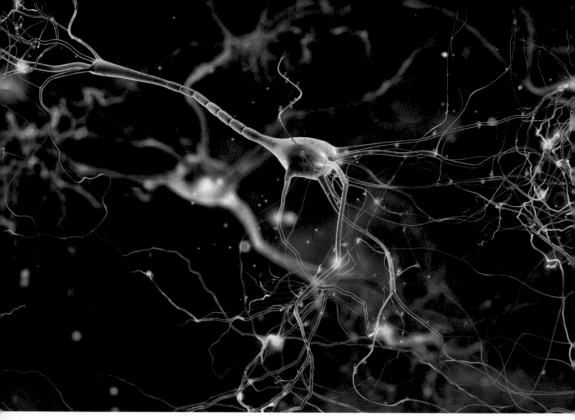

Doctors are not sure what exactly causes gender dysphoria. They believe hormones and neurochemicals may play a part.

come into the womb. These hormonal changes affect the presentation of primary and secondary sex characteristics.

Hormone changes that may lead to gender dysphoria can also be influenced by a rare medical condition called congenital adrenal hyperplasia (CAH). CAH is a condition in which the adrenal glands do not produce certain hormones. These hormones are partially responsible for regulating a person's metabolism, blood pressure, and immune system. In addition to these essential functions, CAH also affects other systems such as cortisol production and androgens.

Cortisol is sometimes called the stress hormone. Cortisol is a hormone made in the adrenal glands above the kidneys. The body releases extra cortisol in times of stress. This often results in increased blood pressure and rapid breathing. But cortisol is always at work in the body regulating blood pressure and blood sugar levels. When a person has CAH, their body does not produce enough cortisol. This can result in mood swings and sudden weight loss.

In contrast, people with CAH produce more androgens than normal, including testosterone. Testosterone is a sex hormone often associated with men. But all people have testosterone in their bodies. Overproduction of androgens can cause early onset of puberty, severe acne, and lower-than-average height. In assigned-female individuals, raised testosterone levels can also cause a deeper voice and facial hair growth. These symptoms, along with others associated with CAH, can cause feelings of gender dysphoria.

CAH can sometimes cause ambiguous genital formation. For example, if a baby with XX chromosomes is born with genitals that resemble a penis, the parents may choose to raise the child as a male. A study looked at 250 CAH patients and how comfortable they were with their gender. Of those 250 individuals, 33 were raised male. At the conclusion of the study, 12.1 percent of the individuals raised as male reported severe gender identity problems. In contrast, only 5.2 percent of the individuals who were raised as female reported issues with gender identity. The authors of the study concluded that all infants born with CAH should be assigned female.

Environmental factors, such as being raised with strict gender roles, could also influence a child's chance of developing GD in adolescence. However, these factors are not well understood. Few comprehensive, long-term studies have been started or completed. Researchers admit that more studies are needed before any conclusions can be drawn.

NEUROCHEMICALS

Every person produces neurochemicals. These chemicals trigger responses in the body. Neurochemicals such as endorphins affect how people feel. Endorphins create a feeling of happiness or euphoria. Some people explain it as a "natural high." Endorphins give people a feeling of well-being. These chemicals are also a natural pain reliever. They are important in establishing reward centers in the brain. The brain recognizes that certain things feel good, and it wants to do them more.

But for people who do not identify with the gender they were assigned at birth, looking in the mirror can be a painful and stressful experience. The brain releases cortisol, causing a stress response. People with gender dysphoria ease these stress responses when they dress and are perceived as their correct gender. Their brains produce more endorphins. But if a person dresses as their expressed gender and is not accepted, feelings of dysphoria can intensify. The need for research and understanding is crucial. As Dr. Rosenthal further explained, "Why do [researchers] do this work? Because we know if people are not acknowledged in who they are, there is a tremendous amount of suffering and risk."[11]

> "We know if people are not acknowledged in who they are, there is a tremendous amount of suffering and risk."[11]
>
> – Dr. Steve Rosenthal, professor of pediatrics

Those risks include severe anxiety and depression, post-traumatic stress disorder (PTSD), and substance use disorders. For example, experiencing anxiety as a result of gender dysphoria can cause an increase of cortisol in the system. Chronic stress causes many different issues. Unfortunately, sometimes people cope with stress in unhealthy ways. People cannot see these chemicals and hormones. But they can see their effects. For one parent, helping her transgender child, Sam, socially and medically transition created a big difference. She explained:

> In fourth grade, we worked with Sam's school to put out a letter to his classmates' parents, announcing his social transition into male pronouns and bathrooms.
> After his social transition, Sam's life blossomed. . . .
> The first longitudinal study of transgender children, "Young Adult Psychological Outcome after Puberty Suppression and Gender Reassignment," found that treated transgender youth are at least as mentally healthy as the general population. And in fact our son today is a happy, well-adjusted, and popular eighth grader.[12]

With support from his parents and classmates, Sam was able to transition. Treatments such as Sam's help prevent the creation of unhealthy coping mechanisms.

WHO EXPERIENCES GENDER DYSPHORIA?

Gender dysphoria is complex. Many people experience the disorder. Some people think only transgender people have gender dysphoria. However, this is an overgeneralization. Transgender people make up a large percentage of people with gender dysphoria.

Some activists use *trans* instead of *transgender*. *Trans* is more inclusive of nonbinary identities. It is an umbrella term that encompasses many different gender identities. It does not describe sexual identities like *lesbian*, *gay*, or *bisexual*. *Gender variance* includes trans identities as well as gender nonconforming people.

Gender identity and sexual orientation are different. Both are addressed in the acronym *LGBTQ*.

Some trans people use the word *queer* to describe their gender and sexual orientation. *Queer* used to be used as a slur against LGBTQ people. For this reason, there are many older people in the LGBTQ communities who will not use the word to describe themselves. Modern definitions of *queer* make it a term that encompasses all aspects of identity, including gender identity and sexual orientation.

GLSEN is an organization that works to create safer schools for LGBTQ students. The name originally stood for Gay, Lesbian, and Straight Education Network. It was simplified to GLSEN to be more inclusive.

Ose Arheghan was the 2017 GLSEN student advocate of the year. The then-seventeen-year-old nonbinary high school student described why language and a term like queer is so important. They said:

> Not everybody knows what things mean, and so when we talk about queerness, that means a lot of different things to different people. It can mean queerness in terms of sexuality, it can mean queerness in terms of gender, it can mean queerness in terms of being other than cis-heteronormativity. And so, when it comes to language, the idea of using terms to pinpoint exactly what somebody identifies as, what somebody embodies as a person— it's so important.[13]

Having the language to talk about identity is one of the first ways people combat gender dysphoria. Naming a feeling helps the person manage that feeling and seek help for discomfort.

Gender nonconforming people may identify as cisgender. However, their outward appearance and mannerisms could be interpreted by others as being contrary to their gender identity. Just as transgender and nonbinary people are misgendered by strangers and sometimes family, gender nonconforming people can have similar experiences. For example, a cisgender woman may present in a gender nonconforming way. She may be read by strangers as a man. This is an example of misgendering.

It is important to note that not all gender variant people experience dysphoria. Gender identity and expression take on many forms. Genetic disorders, hormone imbalances, and trans identities are all just part of a larger picture. There is not one single predictor or cause of gender dysphoria.

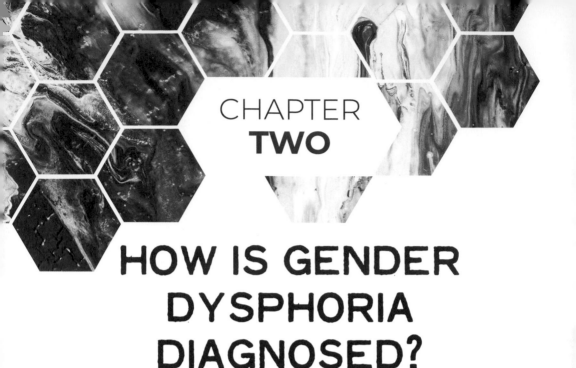

CHAPTER
TWO

HOW IS GENDER DYSPHORIA DIAGNOSED?

Diagnosing gender dysphoria can be complicated. There are several reasons for this, including a high rate of co-occurrence with other mental disorders. The medical community has a long history of treating gender and sexual identity variance as a disease. Treating a natural occurrence as a disease is called *pathologizing*. As a result, many trans people distrust the medical community.

CLASSIFYING MENTAL DISORDERS

The United States didn't always have a system for diagnosing mental illnesses. The 1840 US census was the first time the United States tried to track the rate of mental illness. It tracked the number of people identified with the condition of "idiocy/insanity."[14] By 1880, there were seven mental health classifications available on the census. While getting a number of people who were identified as mentally ill was important, the lists from the census had no real clinical use. Medical professionals realized there needed to be a standardized diagnosis for disorders.

Transgender people sometimes face discrimination from health care professionals. This can make it difficult to seek treatment.

In 1917, the American Medico-Psychological Association worked to create a book of statistics from mental hospitals. The purpose was to see if there were similarities in symptoms across the whole population of people in mental hospitals. This was a good start toward creating a more clinical manual. However, the result was still geared more toward classification than to being a useful diagnostic tool. In 1921, the American Medico-Psychological Association became the American Psychiatric Association (APA). The APA continued to improve its methods.

Soon after changing its name, the APA teamed up with the New York Academy of Medicine. Their goal was to create a classification system for mental illness that doctors could use. The system they developed was included in the first edition of the American Medical Association's

Standard Classified Nomenclature of Disease in 1933. This manual listed many different diseases and their symptoms. However, the manual was not exhaustive. Only severe mental illnesses and neurological disorders were included in the first edition.

After World War II (1939–1945), the United States Army created its own classification of mental disorders. Army officials wanted a way to track the effects of war on soldiers. This classification influenced the World Health Organization (WHO) when it published its sixth edition of the International Classification of Diseases (ICD-6) in 1948. This was the first edition in which mental disorders were included.

The APA used the ICD-6 to create a useful diagnostic tool for doctors. It wasn't enough to have a classification system. There had to be a way for doctors to look at a manual and be able to confidently diagnose a person suffering from a mental disorder. The APA looked at a study conducted by Thomas V. Moore in 1930. According to a review published in the *Annual Review of Clinical Psychology*,

> Moore gathered data on 367 psychotic patients from two mental institutions in the Washington, DC area. . . . These symptom groupings corresponded to similar diagnostic constructs common in inpatient psychiatry at the time and provided evidence in support of grouping symptoms into identifiable syndromes.[15]

The way Moore studied the patients is still used by researchers today. His results helped to influence the writers of the first *Diagnostic and Statistical Manual of Mental Disorders (DSM)*. In 1952, the APA published the first edition of the *DSM*. Finally, doctors had a standardized set of symptoms for mental disorders.

THE *DSM*

The *DSM* is a tool used by medical professionals. The manual is a book of possible diagnosable mental disorders with symptoms and diagnostic criteria. The *DSM* is always changing. That means that symptoms, names of disorders, and treatments are changing, too. As of 2019, the most-current edition was the *DSM-5*. This is the fifth edition of the *DSM*. Between the first edition in 1952 and the publication of the fifth edition in 2013, many new disorders have been added, and several have been taken away.

Homosexuality itself was removed from the *DSM* in 1973. However, the APA established a different disorder in its place: sexual orientation disturbance. Effectively, this kept same-sex attraction within the *DSM* until the revision of the third edition (*DSM-III-R*) was published in 1987. This decision reflected a change in the viewpoint of mental health professionals. They recognized that variance in sexual orientation was normal, as sex researcher Alfred Kinsey noted in 1948 when he wrote, "[People] do not represent two discrete populations, heterosexual and homosexual. The world is not to be divided into sheep and goats. . . . The living world is a continuum in each and every one of its aspects."[16] But it would take much longer for professionals to see gender on a continuum.

> "[People] do not represent two discrete populations, heterosexual and homosexual."[16]
>
> – *Dr. Alfred Kinsey, sex researcher*

Gender variation has been included as a diagnosable mental disorder since the *DSM-II* was published in 1968. It has been classified under several different names and categories. Originally, people were diagnosed with transsexualism. Transsexualism was considered a sexual deviation

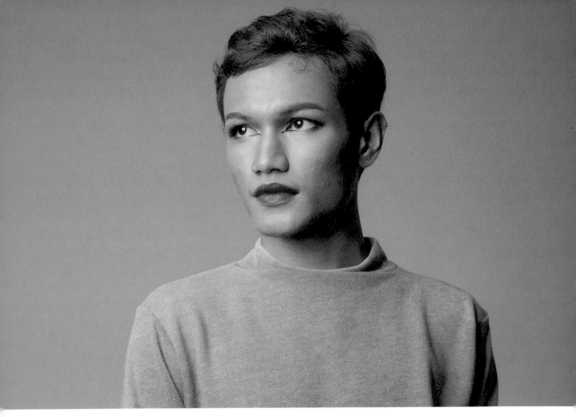

Gender dysphoria was previously called gender identity disorder. The name was changed when mental health professionals created the *DSM-5*.

and, like homosexuality, was seen as treatable. These definitions were often influenced by the societal and cultural norms of the time.

In the *DSM-III-R*, transsexualism was renamed to Gender Identity Disorders (GID). Eventually, all gender variance was diagnosed under this category. GID was a catch-all for any deviation from a cis-normative gender presentation. GID pathologized gender variant people. There was a significant stigma attached to individuals diagnosed with GID, sometimes even from medical professionals.

In theory, having a diagnosis of a disorder from the *DSM* should have allowed trans and GNC people to access gender-affirmative therapies such as hormone treatment through their insurance networks. But this was not often the case. Gender variant people were often mocked or turned away by the doctors who were supposed to be helping them. A change was needed.

The APA is constantly working to update the *DSM*. However, those changes can take a long time to be implemented. An update for the *DSM-IV* into the *DSM-5* was proposed in 2000. A committee was formed in 2007. But the *DSM-5* was not published until 2013.

LGBTQ-rights activists were excited about one important update to the *DSM-5*. GID was renamed *gender dysphoria*. The key difference between the two is that GD does not pathologize a person's gender identity. The person is not disordered. Doctors need to treat the way gender dysphoria manifests, not the condition itself.

Psychiatrist Jack Drescher was a member of the subcommittee that worked on the changes to the *DSM* relating to gender identity. In response to the change, Drescher commented:

> All psychiatric diagnoses occur within a cultural context. We know there is a whole community of people out there who are not seeking medical attention and live between the two binary categories. We wanted to send the message that the therapist's job isn't to pathologize.[17]

> **"The therapist's job isn't to pathologize."[17]**
>
> *– Psychiatrist Jack Drescher*

This change was a welcome one within the trans and GNC communities. Dana Beyer, a committee member for the Washington Psychiatric Society, said the change shifts how trans people are viewed in society. In an interview with the Associated Press, Beyer commented:

A [person] can't go out and say all trans people are mentally ill because if you are not dysphoric, that can't be diagnosed from afar. It no longer matters what your body looks like, what you want to do to it, all of that is irrelevant as far as the APA goes.[18]

Part of the reason for the name change was that the term *dysphoria* was already in use within GNC and trans communities. Gender variant people were already familiar with the term and the feelings that it describes. Diagnoses of gender dysphoria could be validating instead of pathologizing.

The thing that matters for the APA is how a person feels about their gender, and whether that feeling causes distress. Before the release of the *DSM-5*, the APA released a position statement on transgender health care. It stated that affirmative care was imperative to the well-being of trans and gender nonconforming people. The APA wrote that trans people were subject to "significant discrimination, prejudice, and the potential for victimization from violent hate crimes, as well as denial of many basic civil rights, protections, and access to health care, to the severe detriment of their mental health."[19]

However, social stigma surrounding gender variance continues to be an obstacle for gender nonconforming and trans individuals. There are activists within these communities who believe GD should be taken out of the *DSM*. Because variance in gender is normal within a population, these activists believe a GD diagnosis does more harm than good.

DIAGNOSING GENDER DYSPHORIA

There is no gene that can predict gender dysphoria. The human body doesn't carry an extra chemical that causes dysphoria. Therefore, doctors must rely on surveys to gauge whether their patient fits the criteria for a GD diagnosis.

The criteria for a GD diagnosis are different for children than for adolescents and adults. Adolescents and adults must show two of six possible symptoms. The symptoms must appear for six months and be accompanied by significant distress. Children must show six of eight possible symptoms. Their symptoms must appear with problems in functioning and distress for six months. The broader symptoms can be summarized into three major categories: A person states they want to be a different sex. A person has feelings of distress or stigma associated with their assigned sex. A person chooses activities that lessen that distress.

DOES GENDER DYSPHORIA BELONG IN THE *DSM*?

There are many reasons gender dysphoria is included as a mental disorder in the *DSM-5*. One of the reasons is that gender dysphoria has a strong co-occurrence with other mental disorders, such as anxiety and depression. But many people are beginning to think that including gender dysphoria as a mental disorder does more harm than good.

Critics of including GD in the *DSM* look at how cultures around the world view gender. Historically, the binary of male and female didn't exist. Hundreds of cultures have three or more distinct genders. Rather than being considered disordered, the individuals who are neither male nor female are respected within their society.

These critics argue that there is no historical reason to medicalize trans and nonbinary people. The medical community itself agrees that variance in sexuality and gender is normal. However, some medical professionals say that including gender dysphoria in the *DSM* can provide necessary medical and psychiatric coverage. But they also admit that access to services is limited in the United States. Trans advocates and medical professionals alike are divided on whether including gender dysphoria in the *DSM* is more helpful than harmful. Some suggest that taking GD out of the *DSM* will not get rid of the stigma. Stigma is associated with society. It will take much longer to change the way people see gender.

The way these symptoms show up in gender dysphoric people varies between children and adults. In adults, doctors rely on how patients describe their feelings toward their gender. Adults may want to get rid of their primary or secondary sex characteristics. They may also, in turn, want the primary and secondary sex characteristics of a different gender. In an article for *BuzzFeed*, artist and writer Liz explains:

> Everything reminding me of my body is like a very big punch on my face, whether it's things I notice on me (body features, voice, etc.) or things that I notice I don't have but cis women do. I feel like every day, every minute I have to struggle, and I feel like all of these things are dragging me down, threatening my mental health.

THE SOCIALIZATION OF GENDER

Children learn early in their lives what society expects of them. These expectations are not just about moral behavior but about their behavior as a certain gender. Children hear the messages that adults spread in television, music, schools, and at home, and they quickly realize what is the "right" way to be a boy or a girl.

For some parents, the socialization of a child's gender begins before birth. Expecting parents paint rooms in "boy" or "girl" colors. They have gender-reveal parties. For others, it begins at birth. Parents are asked whether they have a boy or a girl. They receive toys, clothes, and blankets that are typically assigned to whatever answer the parents give. These children grow up in an environment with certain toys and clothes and colors without initially knowing what any of it means.

As children grow, the adults in their life serve as models of how to act. Many children get their first lessons in what it means to be a boy or a girl from their parents. But children also get these lessons from their peers and media. A child on the playground may say a certain toy is only for girls or some sport is only for boys. A TV show may have a character who has very rigid gender roles. These are small moments that have a huge influence on how children understand the society they live in and what expectations society has for them.

Yet, at the same time, I have to put on a mask and pretend everything's all right, so nobody knows what's happening under the surface.[20]

In addition to wanting to look like a different gender, adults may also want to be treated as a different gender. Adults may go out of their way to be perceived as another gender. This is a way to lessen their feelings of anxiety. Validation lessens anxiety and feelings of dysphoria.

Children do not necessarily have the vocabulary to talk about their gender. But they are very aware of the difference between how other people see them and how they see themselves. Therefore, many children are vocal about these inconsistencies and their desire to remedy them.

While adults may try to hide their discomfort, children often do not. They may insist they are a different gender. They might prefer wearing clothes typical of the opposite gender. They might choose toys or games that are stereotypically enjoyed by the opposite gender. In an interview with CBS, a young girl, Zoey, explained how she hated when people thought she was a boy. She said, "I would be like, 'No, I'm not a boy. I'm a girl. You know, like, I like the color pink, I scream like a girl. I act like a girl. I breathe like a girl. I'm not a boy.'"[21]

Untreated gender dysphoria in children can have a huge impact. GD causes people to isolate themselves. In children, this can lead to school avoidance, especially in later school years. For youth who do not identify with the gender on their birth certificate, being made to change in a locker room or use the restroom of the wrong gender can be a stressful and sometimes harmful experience. Over time, youth may develop anxiety and depression and may begin acting out or feel suicidal.

Gender dysphoria is often co-occurring with other mental disorders. Anxiety and depression are the two most common co-occurring disorders.

CO-OCCURRENCE

The nature of gender dysphoria as a disorder often means that other mental disorders occur alongside it. This co-occurrence is called *comorbidity*. Comorbidity is common in mental disorders. The 2002 US National Comorbidity Survey showed that 51 percent of people with major depressive disorder also had at least one other disorder. Further, disorders left untreated can make the symptoms of other disorders worse, or create more disorders, such as substance abuse, in the future.

Anxiety and depression are commonly comorbid with gender dysphoria. Depression as a result of GD comes from a belief that a person's outward appearance will never look like what the person imagines. Anxiety comes from the perceptions and judgments of peers. It is as important for doctors to treat these disorders as it is to treat the gender dysphoria. Without comprehensive treatment plans, people who live with GD may struggle to cope in healthy ways with their symptoms.

EXPERIENCES WITH MEDICAL PROFESSIONALS

The pathologizing of gender variance and sexuality harmed the LGBTQ community. In the early twentieth century, doctors believed removing parts of a person's brain (lobotomies) could cure a variety of mental disorders. Many LGBTQ people were hospitalized. Today, parents might send their LGBTQ children to conversion therapists who try to change the child's gender or sexual identity. As a result, LGBTQ people often distrust the medical community at large.

Many things have changed in the medical community since the years of lobotomies. But transgender and gender nonconforming people often still have negative experiences with doctors. One of the largest reasons for this is that many doctors do not have any knowledge about transgender health care needs.

A 2014 study of gynecologists found that 80 percent of them did not have specific training for transgender patients. Pre-operative transmasculine people still need regular gynecological care. However, many of these people report being misgendered or outright denied care. Similarly, a study published in 2017 about endocrinologists' knowledge of transgender health needs also showed a lack of knowledge. While 86 percent of respondents reported treating a transgender person,

80 percent said they had never received formal training for the specific needs of those patients. All gender variant people who use hormones as part of their treatment of dysphoria see an endocrinologist. It is vital that medical professionals know how to care for their patients.

Ignorance or personal biases can lead to unnecessary questioning. In 2013, Tanya Walker was coughing up blood. She went to the emergency room. But instead of treating her, her doctor asked her about her genitals. The fifty-three-year-old transgender woman said, "It seemed like they weren't going to treat me unless I told them what genitals I had."[22]

> "It seemed like they weren't going to treat me unless I told them what genitals I had."[22]
>
> – Tanya Walker, on her experience in the emergency room

In addition to invasive questioning, trans patients have been harassed and even denied care by physicians. A 2018 report from the Human Rights Watch, an organization that studies human rights across the globe, showed that despite progress toward equality, transgender patients still faced discrimination. The report showed that 29 percent of transgender respondents said they had been denied care. Twenty-one percent said doctors used discriminatory language. Discriminatory language includes refusing to use the person's correct name and pronoun. For one teen, his doctor continued to refer to him as a girl even while giving him his testosterone injection.

For many trans people, these experiences and reports do not inspire confidence in medical professionals. As a result, trans people are more likely to avoid or delay medical care. In a survey done for a 2016 paper, 30 percent of adult transgender respondents said they avoid seeking medical care. The paper also showed that transgender patients were four times more likely to delay necessary treatments due to a fear of discrimination. These numbers are even higher for trans youth.

A study of transgender teens in Canada found that 68 percent of trans teens ages fourteen to eighteen avoided mental health care, and 34 percent avoided getting physical care, even if it was necessary. Elizabeth Saewyc is a nursing professor and one of the authors of the study. She said the study highlighted the need for doctors to be knowledgeable about the health care needs of transgender youth. In an interview, she said:

> Trans youth have higher risk for negative health outcomes due to stigma and discrimination, so knowing that they don't access health care even when they need to is concerning. The responsibility lies with us—with health professionals, health educators, and policymakers—to improve our competency in transgender health and ensure our trans patients can have confidence in the health care they receive.[23]

But the study also had a bright side. PhD candidate Beth Clark noted that "young people who were more comfortable discussing trans health care needs with their family doctors reported higher levels of mental health and health overall."[24] This trend reinforces the benefit of doctors and mental health professionals who practice gender-affirmative care.

"Trans youth have higher risk for negative health outcomes due to stigma and discrimination."[23]

– Elizabeth Saewyc,
nursing professor

CHAPTER
THREE

WHAT IS LIFE LIKE WITH GENDER DYSPHORIA?

Living with gender dysphoria can be difficult. Both adults and youth struggle with coping in positive ways with the stress from GD. People living with GD may experience self-harm tendencies, negative reactions from family and peers, and difficulty accessing necessary medical services. All of these things can have adverse consequences.

INTERNAL STRUGGLES

For people who live with gender dysphoria, their bodies cause them anxiety. This anxiety can cause people to hurt themselves physically and emotionally. In an interview with *BuzzFeed*, one respondent explained that dysphoria is much more complicated than just discomfort. They wrote:

> [I] struggle with dermatillomania, or skin-picking. Every day, I cave in to the feeling that I need to pick and rub my skin. Through some research, I found out that these types of disorders are often associated with body dysphoria and dysmorphia. . . . Dysphoria

Dermatillomania is the compulsion to pick or rub at the skin. People with GD may struggle with compulsive behaviors such as dermatillomania as a result of their dysphoria.

is so much more than just feeling uncomfortable—it can have a major impact on a person's everyday life.[25]

People with gender dysphoria may find it difficult to do daily tasks, such as managing hygiene. Because of the distress their bodies cause, people may avoid showering. Showering requires acknowledging the parts of a body that a dysphoric person is most uncomfortable with. People have to find solutions. For one person, they found a way to navigate around their discomfort. In an interview, they said, "Before taking any clothes off, I turn on

"Dysphoria is so much more than just feeling uncomfortable."[25]

– *An anonymous person with gender dysphoria*

Many transmasculine people use chest binders to reduce the appearance of breasts. But binding too much can lead to health problems.

the water really hot so that all the mirrors in the bathroom are fogged up and I can shower and get dressed without seeing my reflection."[26]

Other people dissociate. For some people, this means they do not recognize their body as their own. *BuzzFeed* asked people to describe their dysphoria. One respondent wrote:

My mind copes with dysphoria in strange ways. I am a transmasculine person, and I almost always feel disconnected from my body, like I don't have one or like I'm not even in my body. Because my brain doesn't seem to recognize my body as my own, I don't feel intense dysphoria about what seems "wrong" about it.[27]

Dissociation is a way for the brain to cope with the mismatch between identity and appearance. Some psychologists define the condition as a defense mechanism.

People who are assigned female, but do not identify as a girl, may choose to use chest binders to minimize the appearance of breasts. This can be a way for people to limit feelings of dysphoria. As one nonbinary trans person, Naomhan, said in an interview, "The first time I put on a binder . . . I remember looking down at my chest and then into the mirror, feeling euphoria at how happy it made me feel." However, some people bind for too many hours. As Naomhan later explained, "I couldn't take my binder off except to sleep. It would be the first thing I put on when I woke up in the morning, and I would feel dysphoric even sitting at home without my binder on."[28] But doctors say this can be dangerous.

> "I would feel dysphoric even sitting at home without my binder on."[28]
>
> – Naomhan, a nonbinary trans person, on using chest binders

Few medical studies have been conducted to study the effects of binding. But the Binding Health Project created an anonymous survey of 1,800 assigned-female-at-birth (AFAB) people who bound their chests. The survey measured how many negative outcomes were associated with chest binding. Researchers looked at different variables to see what the causes of the negative outcomes were. They found that 97 percent of respondents reported at least 1 of 28 possible negative outcomes associated with chest binding. Those individuals who bound their chest daily averaged 22 negative outcomes. The most common side effect was

HEALTHY COPING MECHANISMS

Coping mechanisms are the ways people choose to deal with stressors. Not all coping mechanisms are healthy. People who have gender dysphoria are more likely to find unhealthy coping mechanisms such as substance abuse and self-harm than non–gender dysphoric people. People with gender dysphoria often express wanting to get away from the feelings that come up in association with their bodies.

One of the most important things that people who live with gender dysphoria can do is find healthy coping mechanisms. Therapists often help people find and create healthy coping skills. These tools include a variety of things. Some are as simple as listening to music or reading a book. People can go for a walk, or focus on their breathing for a few minutes. Some therapists recommend people with gender dysphoria keep a journal. Other coping mechanisms take more time, like building a community of other trans and nonbinary people. Creating and practicing healthy coping skills takes time.

back pain, with nearly 54 percent of respondents reporting it. There were even several reports of fractured ribs due to chest binding. Other side effects include overheating and chest pain. For people who bind, pain is an unwanted by-product of trying to ease their discomfort.

Despite these dangers, the respondents were unwilling to stop binding. The authors of the study released a report shortly after the study was published. It read:

Based on our preliminary analysis, for most participants, binding was a positive experience and led to improvements in mood and self-esteem, minimized gender dysphoria, anxiety, and depression, and helped them to feel in control of their bodies. In fact, some reported that a positive impact on emotional and behavioral health makes the physical discomfort of binding worth it.[29]

Many of the respondents reported that they did not seek medical attention, even when they were in pain. One of the reasons for this is that chest binding is not well-understood in the medical community. One trans man, Dylan, said he didn't go to the doctor because "the doctor is just going to tell me to stop doing what I'm doing that hurts me. I don't see the point."[30] For him, the discomfort from binding was worth feeling more comfortable with his appearance.

Many trans and gender nonconforming people who have gender dysphoria intentionally engage in self-harm. One study found that trans youth were significantly more likely to engage in self-harm and attempt suicide than their cisgender peers. Researchers looked at the medical records of ninety-six transgender youth with gender dysphoria, ages twelve to twenty-two. While this study was small, the sample was representative of the nearly 500 transgender patients the Transgender Health Clinic at Cincinnati Children's Hospital worked with between 2013 and 2016. The study showed that 30 percent of transgender youth attempted suicide at least once. Rates of self-injury were even higher. Nearly 42 percent of patients reported a history of self-harm, such as cutting. These rates were higher among transgender men than trans women.

Dr. Claire Peterson, a psychologist at Cincinnati Children's Hospital, led the study. When the results were published, she said:

Our study provides further evidence for the at-risk nature of transgender youth and emphasizes that mental health providers and physicians working with this population need to be aware of these challenges. Dissatisfaction with one's appearance and the drive to look different from one's sex assigned at birth is central to gender dysphoria—the feeling that your gender identity is different from that at birth.[31]

Being denied access to the restroom corresponding to their gender can cause transgender people to skip school. It can also lead to health problems.

In addition to physical injury, the study also found increases in other mental disorders and atypical behavior. Nearly 60 percent of the study's participants had another diagnosed mental disorder. Twenty-three percent of youth in the study had been suspended or expelled from school, and 17 percent repeated at least one grade.

One of the reasons that trans youth are more likely to repeat a grade is because they are more likely to avoid school. Trans and gender nonconforming youth who have gender dysphoria try to present themselves as their true gender. But not all schools are supportive of trans and GNC students. External factors such as school climate can have a negative impact on gender dysphoric youth.

EXTERNAL STRUGGLES

One of the biggest hurdles people with gender dysphoria must overcome is the stress of how other people see them. The desire to pass as their true gender can raise anxiety levels. One writer, Serena Sonoma, is a twenty-four-year-old trans woman. On assignment for the *Daily Dot*, Sonoma writes about her experience with dysphoria and trying to navigate the world:

> When gender dysphoria hits, it packs a punch.
>
> It can come while I'm in the middle of reading a book, a sudden unsettling feeling of not being quite myself. Maybe I recognize that my hands are too big, as I flip to the next page. Maybe I study every part of my face after I shower and clear the foggy mirror, wishing some features were softer and others not quite there. As a transgender woman, my body is conditioned by society to look a certain way. Maybe my breasts could be a little bigger, my voice a little more lilted, my hips slightly wider. It also goes beyond the scope of just physical traits—forms of micro-aggressions can also trigger gender dysphoria.[32]

> **"When gender dysphoria hits, it packs a punch."[32]**
>
> *– Serena Sonoma, a twenty-four-year-old trans woman*

Microaggressions are the small, sometimes unintentional acts people do that create an unsafe or discriminatory environment for minority populations. For trans people, calling people with vaginas "real women" is a microaggression. It invalidates trans women and ignores trans men's experiences. Asking a person if they have medically transitioned is another example. Even if the question is posed without malicious intent, it is invasive. Microaggressions also include asking what a person's birth name is or telling a person they are in the wrong bathroom.

According to the National Center for Transgender Equality (NCTE), 60 percent of transgender students have been denied access to the correct bathroom or locker room. Students are made to change in locker rooms that are inconsistent with their gender identity. Many are either told they need to use the restroom that matches their sex marker on their birth certificate, or they are forced to use a single stall restroom in the nurse's office.

Due to these restrictions, trans and gender nonconforming students are more likely to avoid school. For those students who do attend school, studies show that 70 percent of students avoid using bathrooms. Youth may choose to either "hold it" or limit their liquid consumption so they don't have to use the bathroom. These choices can lead to several health problems. Trans and GNC students are more likely to get urinary tract infections. Limiting liquids can lead to dehydration.

In 2017, Education Secretary Betsy DeVos reversed former US president Barack Obama's protections for transgender students' use of the bathroom that corresponds to their identity. In response, multiple advocacy groups urged DeVos to change the policy. One of these groups was the Movement Advancement Project (MAP), a research organization for equality. MAP's executive director, Ineke Mushovic, wrote:

> On the surface, the argument is about bathrooms, but at a deeper level, it is about whether or not transgender students will be included in our public education system. Put simply, if transgender students cannot safely access a bathroom, they cannot safely attend school.[33]

Not only are students unable to access restrooms that they feel comfortable in, but many schools do not have comprehensive anti-bullying and nondiscrimination policies in place for trans students. This means that trans students are at an increased risk for bullying. Without harassment policies, trans students are not protected from their peers.

Many trans youth feel unsafe. A 2017 report from MAP and GLSEN estimated that there are 150,000 trans students in the United States. In a nationwide survey, 75 percent of trans students felt unsafe at school because of their gender presentation. Outside of school, family relationships can be strained when a person comes out as trans or nonbinary. Unsupportive families can increase distress and lead to other mental disorders such as anxiety, depression, and self-injury.

Mental health professionals recommend that all parents use gender-affirmative practices. These include supporting a child's choices in clothing that supports their identity, requiring respect within the family, and defending a child from negative comments. Parents often need help learning how to understand and support their trans or nonbinary child. Psychologists often recommend family therapy for parents to learn these skills.

> "If transgender students cannot safely access a bathroom, they cannot safely attend school."[33]
>
> – *Ineke Mushovic, executive director of MAP*

The impact that non-affirmative parenting has on gender variant youth is wide. Youth who are emotionally or physically abused by their parents may develop PTSD. Trans and nonbinary youth are more likely to run away from home than their cisgender peers. Most often, this is due to mistreatment from parents or guardians.

PTSD is a serious mental health concern that some trans and nonbinary individuals develop as a result of being subjected to certain

Having a supportive family makes dealing with gender dysphoria easier. Psychologists often suggest family therapy to help families work together to be supportive.

events and situations, such as abuse or chronic discrimination. Although PTSD is often associated with soldiers and combat, PTSD can arise as a result of many other traumatic life events or repeated stressful experiences. A 2012 study showed that transgender people were up to 3.9 times more likely to develop PTSD than their cisgender peers.

PTSD can be caused by childhood trauma such as abuse. But it can also develop over time as people hear over and over that their gender identity isn't real or doesn't matter. Trauma can stay hidden for years until a moment triggers an unconscious memory and reaction from a person with PTSD. In an interview with *Teen Vogue*, psychologist Dara Hoffman-Fox explained how symptoms of PTSD can show up. She said:

The symptoms of both PTSD and Complex PTSD experienced as a result of trauma during youth are oftentimes revealed during adulthood through intimate relationships with others. Issues relating to abandonment, trust, attachment, and codependency are common, as well as having an inability to emotionally regulate what tend to be "normal" stressful relationship challenges.[34]

Hoffman-Fox goes on to explain that unconscious memories of trauma can show up seemingly out of nowhere: "Environmental stressors can lead to being triggered, such as being in certain situations that end up feeling very unsafe."[35] These environmental factors could include a smell, a sound, or an object that reminds the person of the past trauma.

Dana Breyer is a transgender advocate. She was diagnosed with PTSD. Talking about the diagnosis, she said she didn't realize it was due to her identity. Breyer explained:

> I was diagnosed with PTSD over a quarter century ago, having been raped and tortured as an adolescent. I never directly related that to being trans, nor did my physicians. It was actually related to my reproductive intersex status. . . . I also think a critical issue is that PTSD in these cases is not derived from trans status itself, but the abuse that comes from being perceived as trans.[36]

SOCIETAL STRUGGLES

Gender variant people living with gender dysphoria also experience struggles related to discrimination against them in society. These struggles affect the way people with GD navigate their world. People with GD have difficulty accessing medical services and are at an increased risk of being the victim of a hate crime.

Hate-crime rates against transgender people are higher than the national average. A hate crime is an act of violence against a person for

> "PTSD in these cases is not derived from trans status itself, but the abuse that comes from being perceived as trans."[36]
>
> *– Transgender advocate Dana Breyer*

a trait that the person cannot change. The Human Rights Campaign published a study in 2018 of fatal hate crimes against trans people. It found the vast majority of hate crimes against trans people happen to trans women. Trans women of color make up 80 percent of trans victims of hate crimes.

Victims of hate crimes are also young. The same study showed that 75 percent of American trans hate crime victims were under the age of thirty-five, and 45 percent of victims lived in the southern United States. These include only known transgender victims of hate crimes. Many hate crimes go unreported due to the high number of people experiencing homelessness who are transgender. Another reason for low reporting is the misgendering of trans people in newspapers and obituaries.

Eight percent of transgender youth who come out to their families are kicked out of the house. A survey of youth experiencing homelessness in New York City showed that the average age that a transgender youth becomes homeless is 13.5 years old. When youth try to access services, some providers do not understand why they need help. In an interview with the *Guardian*, one person said:

> I was living with my parents who were abusive and quite transphobic and at various points they would kick me out for a few weeks to a few months. . . .
> I did call one service provider. They didn't seem to understand that transphobic abuse is a form of abuse, basically saying, "You should work it out, you should go home." . . .

After that, and having heard a lot of horror stories from other trans people who had tried to go to other services, I didn't go to any other services.[37]

Other youth choose not to access services because shelters split residents up by sex. For nonbinary people, this categorization can worsen symptoms of dysphoria because they are neither male nor female. This means that gender variant people who experience homelessness are often without a home for longer than their cisgender peers who experience homelessness. One study noted that transgender youth in New York City often spend more than 50 months homeless. Cisgender peers spend less than 30 months.

A PROTECTED DISABILITY

The Americans with Disabilities Act (ADA) protects people with disabilities from employment discrimination. The ADA originally did not protect people with gender identity disorder (GID). But when the *DSM* removed GID and replaced it with gender dysphoria, the ADA considered the condition a protected disability.

This protection was reinforced in a landmark court ruling in 2017. Kate Blatt is a transgender woman. She worked for a year at Cabela's, a sporting goods store, stocking shelves. She had legally changed her name and dressed in clothes that matched her female gender identity. During her job orientation, she used the women's restroom without issue. However, when she started her job, Cabela's gave her a name tag with the name James on it. Her manager also required her to use the single stall restroom at the front of the store. Blatt was harassed by her coworkers until she was fired in 2007.

Blatt sued Cabela's for Title VII sex discrimination as well as violating the ADA's protection. Blatt claimed that the company did not provide her accommodations for her disability, such as giving her a name tag with her name on it and allowing her to use the restroom that matched her gender identity. A federal district court ruled in her favor in 2017. According to the ruling, the ADA protects Blatt and other people with gender dysphoria because the condition "substantially limits her major life activities of interacting with others, reproducing, and social and occupational functioning."

"Blatt v. Cabela's Retail Inc.," GLAD, May 18, 2017. www.glad.org.

Transgender people are more likely to experience homelessness than their cisgender peers. They may be turned away from shelters based on their biological sex.

The National Center for Transgender Equality (NCTE) estimates that twenty percent of transgender people have been homeless at some point in their lives. NCTE also says transgender people are more likely to be denied gender-affirmative shelters. For example, a trans woman is told she must stay in the men's shelter. For people living with gender dysphoria, being forced to stay in a shelter that goes against their identity can be damaging. Anxiety and depression can worsen. Transgender people experiencing homelessness are more likely to abuse alcohol and drugs as a coping mechanism. Transgender people who are placed in shelters counter to their gender identity face a higher likelihood of being sexually assaulted.

One in two transgender people are victims of sexual violence in their lives. In the general population, 1 in 3 women and 1 in 6 men are victims of sexual violence. A 2011 study found that 12 percent of trans and gender variant youth in grades K–12 were sexually assaulted by peers or staff. The same study showed that 13 percent of transgender African American employees were assaulted at work, and 22 percent of transgender people experiencing homelessness were assaulted while they were staying in shelters.

Poverty and violence are linked. The cycle of poverty means that people who are in poverty tend to stay in poverty. Resources are limited to help trans people get out of the cycle, especially if they have been homeless. Youth homelessness can lead to a gap in education. Finding a job without a high school diploma is difficult. Secure housing without a regular income exists but often has long waiting lists. Transgender and gender variant people who have resource insecurity cannot spend money on getting medical care.

A 2015 survey of 27,000 transgender people in the United States showed that about one-third were living in poverty. Fifteen percent of survey respondents were unemployed. The national average is only about 5 percent. Living in poverty often means that people do not have access to health insurance. Mental health care and other gender-affirmative medical care is expensive. This means many people with gender dysphoria living in poverty cannot access necessary services. Without treatment, studies show that comorbid disorders like depression and anxiety worsen. It is important for the well-being of all people with GD to have access to medical and psychological services.

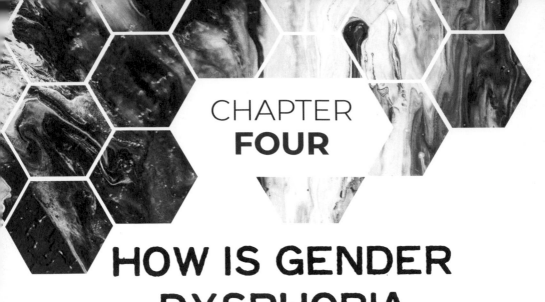

CHAPTER
FOUR

HOW IS GENDER DYSPHORIA TREATED?

Treating gender dysphoria is necessary for trans and gender nonconforming people to feel confident with themselves. Treatment often includes a process called transitioning. Transitioning can be done in many ways. Some people only transition socially. Others transition medically and socially. But treating gender dysphoria can be complicated. People with GD face obstacles such as society's gender stereotypes, comorbid disorders, and financial barriers.

COUNSELING

Much of society does not respect people who do not identify with their assigned sex. Western ideas of binary sex are deeply ingrained in US culture. These values do not recognize other gender identities. Some people try to change a trans or GNC person's gender identity by force. How society sees and treats trans and GNC people can have a huge impact on their gender dysphoria.

Counseling is a major part of treatment for gender dysphoria. There are many types of therapy, including psychotherapy and cognitive behavioral therapy.

Harassment and pressures from society can worsen other mental health disorders. Treating gender dysphoria is a multi-faceted plan. Doctors often prescribe medication to ease symptoms of anxiety and depression. But medication is not enough. Medical professionals recommend that people with GD see a mental health professional as well. This could include group or individual therapy.

There are many different types of therapy. Many people with depression and anxiety use psychotherapy. Psychotherapy is often called talk therapy. People meet one-on-one or in groups with a licensed therapist. Sessions are usually once a week. Patients discuss problems

THE FIGHT AGAINST CONVERSION THERAPY

Conversion therapy isn't true therapy. The practice is meant to change a trans or gay person's identity. Conversion therapy is based on the belief that all people are straight and cisgender. The organizations that practice conversion therapy use false science to back up their claim that people can change their sexual or gender identities. Methods include hypnosis, aversive conditioning, and other methods of talk therapy. Historically, electro-shock treatments and lobotomies have been used.

The problem with conversion therapy isn't just that it doesn't work. Psychologists and other medical professionals agree that conversion therapy is actively harmful, especially for adolescents. People who go through conversion therapy are likely to display signs of anxiety and depression. These people are also likely to attempt suicide and engage in other risky behaviors.

As of 2019, the US federal government does not outlaw conversion therapy. However, several states have passed laws that prohibit licensed counselors from engaging in conversion therapy practices. LGBTQ advocacy groups continue to fight to ban all types of conversion therapy.

they're having in their lives. Therapists listen and give suggestions for how clients could make changes in their thinking or behavior.

According to the APA, 75 percent of people who use psychotherapy show some benefit. Talk therapy is most beneficial for treating depression, anxiety, and trauma. For more severe disorders such as PTSD, other forms of counseling can be helpful. Cognitive behavioral therapy (CBT) is one type. CBT is a more intense form of psychotherapy. These sessions are almost always short-term in nature. They last only a few weeks. The purpose of CBT is to provide active coping mechanisms for negative thinking and responses that patients have learned over time. Patients learn to manage emotions and stressful life situations. After completing CBT, many patients continue to work with other therapists long-term to manage their symptoms.

Dialectical Behavioral Therapy (DBT) is another kind of therapy. DBT helps people whose gender dysphoria causes them to engage in self-harm. Self-harm can include cutting. But it can also include risky behaviors such as drug use. DBT focuses on creating healthy coping mechanisms and teaching life skills that help a person feel safer in their body. Group therapies like CBT and DBT are highly effective for many people. These groups develop close-knit communities that help people feel less alone.

Combining medication and talk therapy is often more effective than a single treatment option. A meta-analysis of fifty-two studies on treatment of depression and anxiety for adults showed that a combination of medication and talk therapy was more effective than one type of treatment. The same can be said for youth with severe anxiety. In a 2017 study, 60 percent of study participants using both medication and therapy were symptom-free in 12 weeks. Only 25 percent of single-therapy participants showed similar outcomes. Therapy and medication can allow people with gender dysphoria to effectively treat their other disorders in order to cope with their GD. Because of the multi-faceted nature of GD, a multi-system approach to treatment is necessary.

SOCIAL TRANSITIONING

Social transition is the process of affirming a person's gender identity without hormones or surgical intervention. The purpose of social transitioning is for people's gender identity to be seen, acknowledged, and respected in public. Social transitioning includes dressing in a way that affirms a person's gender identity, changing their name and pronouns, and using the bathroom that corresponds with their gender identity. All of these things help reinforce the person's identity in public spaces.

People may begin by buying clothes that affirm their gender. They may start by only wearing their new clothes at home. Over time, they may wear them in front of friends, and then in public. Transition takes time. Trans and nonbinary people need to get used to their own feelings about their gender. Then they can get used to the responses of others.

Transfeminine people in particular may feel self-conscious about their lower voice and masculine facial appearance. There are many online resources specifically for transfeminine people to learn makeup and vocal training techniques. Makeup isn't used only for feminizing features. It can be a way for people to express their gender identity. Gender expression takes many different forms. Many gender nonconforming people love experimenting with makeup. Makeup is a way for people to show their individuality.

Trans and GNC people may also choose undergarments to mask certain parts of their anatomy. Transmasculine individuals may use binders. People use binders to minimize the appearance of breasts. Transfeminine people may choose to wear padded bras to create the appearance of larger breasts. These undergarments are important. They allow trans and gender nonconforming people to feel good about themselves. It is important to recognize that not all trans and GNC people want to be seen as the same as cisgender people. But clothing and undergarments help them be seen as a gender other than their assigned sex.

Blending in can be helpful when trans and gender nonconforming people want to use public restrooms. Studies show that allowing trans people to use the bathroom that matches their gender identity minimizes feelings of anxiety and stress. A survey conducted in 2008 and 2009

Transgender people may wear clothing that affirms their gender identity as part of their social transition. They may also choose a new name.

showed that trans people who were denied access to a public restroom also showed an increased likelihood of thinking about suicide. A 2014 study of school climate showed that students who felt unsafe using the bathroom that matched their gender identity also had lower self-esteem and grades when compared with the whole school population. The authors of the study concluded:

> Together, these findings suggest that while identifying as trans may help students, on average, to affirm their sense of self within the broader community, it also exposes students to multiple

barriers of sexism and genderism in successfully accessing both social and educational opportunities in school environments.[38]

Part of social transition often includes changing a person's name. When people decide to change their name, they usually start with friends and family. Then they begin to introduce themselves to coworkers with their true name. For some trans and nonbinary people, birth names can be a reminder of a painful past. Changing their name allows people with gender dysphoria to feel recognized in society.

Actor Rebecca Root says a name is one of the most important parts of a person's identity. In an interview with the magazine *Advocate*, Root says:

"A lot of people don't consider the name. . . . But it is a big deal. It's that moment when you announce yourself to the world in your new identity."[39]

– Actor Rebecca Root

A lot of people don't consider the name. People who are not trans think of possible surgeries . . . and they think about what's beneath the visible physical changes. But it is a big deal. It's that moment when you announce yourself to the world in your new identity.[39]

When people change their name, they may not change their name on their official documents, such as driver's licenses and birth certificates, for months or years. An official name change can be an expensive and multi-step legal process. Many states require a court hearing. Some even require people to publish their name change in the local newspaper, like a birth announcement. In addition to being confusing, there are often filing fees that can cost hundreds of dollars.

The process can take months. Emily Tomaine, a chemist from Pennsylvania, recalls the experience as being complicated. She said:

You have to go through a petition . . . [A]fter that whole process, it took me probably three or four months in between to go through that name-change process. I went to court, I ended up having a big hearing, and I ended up having four lawyers there and other people in the room, who basically get called up to present your case and all the documents.[40]

Despite the challenges and the long process, official name changes often allow people to begin fully living as their true identity in all aspects of their life. Tomaine said she was finally able to change her name at work, where she felt she was living a "half-life." While some people choose to medically transition alongside their social transition, there are many people with gender dysphoria for whom social transition is enough to dissipate feelings of dysphoria.

MEDICAL TRANSITIONING

Like social transitions, medical transitions are about a person feeling confident with themselves. Medical transition physically alters a person's body through surgery or chemical hormones. Dr. Cesar A. Gonzalez is a psychologist at the Mayo Clinic in Rochester, Minnesota. He works with trans and gender variant patients to provide a treatment plan to ease their feelings of dysphoria. While medical transitions alter a person's appearance, Dr. Gonzalez says that transition is not about looks:

Gender transition is less about how people look and more about helping individuals feel congruent with themselves. Some patients don't undergo surgical interventions; for them, taking hormones may be enough. Others want surgery. It's about being open to gender fluidity rather than having a stereotyped idea of the gender binary. . . .

We don't want to go from one gender box to another. Instead, we want to help patients find their own authentic sense of identity—a practice that may or may not include medical intervention to facilitate changes in gender expression. Ultimately, it's all a process.[41]

> "It's about being open to gender fluidity rather than having a stereotyped idea of the gender binary."[41]
>
> – Psychologist Cesar A. Gonzalez on the transition process

According to a 2011 National Transgender Discrimination Survey, 61 percent of trans people chose to medically transition. Thirty-three percent surgically transitioned. Twenty-eight percent used only hormone replacement therapy (HRT).

HRT is the use of estrogen or testosterone to create a physiological change in a person's body. These hormones are used to feminize or masculinize a person's body. All people naturally have both hormones.

Estrogen and testosterone are sex hormones. They create certain physical features in the body. A person who was assigned female at birth typically has more estrogen in their system. This is the reason they grow breasts during puberty. But estrogen is also responsible for storing fat around the hips. Testosterone is created primarily in the testes. Testosterone causes the growth of facial hair. It also works to build muscle mass instead of storing fat. These are traits commonly associated with masculinity.

Gender-dysphoric youth in the early stages of puberty can take a different type of hormone. This hormone blocks the hormones that cause secondary sex characteristics to form. These hormones are called hormone blockers or puberty blockers. While puberty blockers cannot be used indefinitely, these hormones can give trans and gender nonconforming youth time to assess how they want to live as adults. That may mean starting gender-affirming hormones in tandem with the hormone blockers. In cases where a young person chooses not to transition, puberty blockers are stopped.

For youth who are in the later stages of puberty, hormone blockers can stop the progression of puberty. They can also aid HRT for transfeminine teens. Medical estrogen alone usually isn't enough to override testosterone production. Puberty blockers allow the estrogen to become the primary sex hormone instead of testosterone.

Dr. Johanna Olson is the director of the Center for Transyouth Health and Development at Children's Hospital Los Angeles. This medical center specializes in trans youth health care. Olson says that the main goal of hormone blockers is not to stop puberty altogether: "With hormone blockers . . . we can hit the 'pause' button on puberty. . . . We want people to go through their puberty process with their peers."[42] Adults and late-pubescent youth sometimes refer to the effects of hormone replacement therapy as a second puberty. People often experience mood swings. During adolescence, this is typical. This is part of the reason doctors prefer to start hormone therapy for youth during the gender-appropriate time, so they are going through the same emotional upheaval as their peers. Olson used the example of a boy with ovaries. He would have typically started female puberty around the age of nine.

However, male puberty doesn't typically start until age eleven. Doctors would start hormone blockers at the start of female puberty. Then, around the typical age of male puberty, doctors would begin testosterone therapy.

Hormones and hormone blockers both come with some side effects. Testosterone can cause acne, and estrogen can cause tenderness in breasts. Hormone replacement is linked to an increased likelihood of cancer and heart disease. Hormone blockers for youth are shown to potentially cause decreased bone density. This is the reason puberty blockers should not be used without other hormone therapies long-term.

SURGICAL TRANSITIONING

Besides hormones, some people with gender dysphoria choose surgery to change their bodies. While some people say surgeries of this nature are cosmetic, the reality is that these surgeries can ease many of the anxieties a person has regarding their physical anatomy.

Surgical transition includes top and bottom surgeries. Top surgery includes altering the appearance of a person's chest. For transmasculine people, doctors perform a double mastectomy, or removal of both breasts. Transfeminine people often get breast augmentation. Bottom surgery, or gender reassignment surgery, is the process of surgically creating a vagina or penis. Despite the fact that 33 percent of trans people surgically transition, significantly fewer choose both top and bottom surgeries. Approximately 72 percent of trans men say they don't ever want gender reassignment surgery. On the other hand, only 14 percent of trans women say they won't get gender reassignment surgery.

There are several reasons for this. Surgical transitions of any kind are incredibly expensive. For example, top surgery costs approximately

Description	Code	Amount
		87.00
	851000095	174.00
	172001525	37.60
ge	225647700	9.10
te room	...004102	18.12

Not all trans people choose to surgically transition. Surgeries can be expensive, and insurance doesn't always cover procedure costs.

$10,000. Gender reassignment surgery costs upwards of $25,000. Transmasculine people may also need a hysterectomy at an additional cost. A hysterectomy removes the uterus, ovaries, and fallopian tubes. There are further surgeries that some people choose, such as facial-feminizing for transfeminine people. Facial feminization surgery includes reducing the appearance of the Adam's apple. Trans women may also choose to get implants for their lips and cheeks to make their face look rounder and more feminine. Surgeries such as these are considered cosmetic.

While some health insurance programs cover gender reassignment surgery, there are gaps in coverage. Program benefits vary by state. Some trans-inclusive coverage will cover most or all of the cost of medical transitioning. Others will only cover some of it. Depending on the state, denial of trans-inclusive coverage could be an example of sex discrimination. Sex discrimination is illegal. But people must contest potentially unlawful health care plans, which can be a long process. There is no guarantee that patients will get the care they need.

Besides cost, the disparity between masculine and feminine gender reassignment also has to do with the complexity of the surgeries. Creating a vagina from a penis is easier than constructing a penis. This is also why many intersex infants who have genital reconstruction are given vaginas. Constructing a phallus requires taking skin from another area of the body. There is an increased risk of infection and complications for this procedure, which is called phalloplasty.

Despite the risks associated with surgeries, gender reassignment surgery and top surgery can be key for the well-being of many people with gender dysphoria. A 2014 study of trans women showed that 90 percent of women who had undergone gender reassignment said "their expectations for life as a woman were fulfilled postoperatively."

IT TAKES A VILLAGE

Gender dysphoria is a serious medical condition. The rate of comorbidity with other mental disorders is high. Gender dysphoria is linked to severe depression and anxiety in transgender and gender nonconforming people of all ages. While doctors are not sure what the root cause of gender dysphoria is, they have a clear idea of how best to treat it.

Allowing a person to explore their gender identity is critical to their well-being. Gender-affirmative therapy is the best course of action.

Treatment plans need to be multi-faceted in order to treat all aspects of gender dysphoria, from co-occurring disorders to physical appearance.

But treating gender dysphoria is not a journey taken alone. Treatment plans include specialists in a variety of medical fields. Plastic surgeons, mental health professionals, and endocrinologists all work to help a person with gender dysphoria find relief.

It is also important to recognize the role that society plays in gender dysphoria. The ways in which children are socially conditioned in binary gender roles and expressions is harmful to individuals and society. Sex and gender are categories that encompass many different identities and chromosomal configurations.

A cultural shift in how people view gender may be helpful in easing feelings of dysphoria. More and more youth are identifying outside of the

FINDING AND BUILDING COMMUNITY

Building a community of gender-affirming friends isn't just about coping. Trusted and supportive friends help lessen the effects of gender dysphoria. Anxiety and stress about the way a body looks or does not look is less pronounced in spaces where people are supportive. These groups might be GSAs (Gender and Sexuality Alliances or Gay-Straight Alliances) at school. They might also be sports teams or theater castmates. But it is important to recognize the role that social media plays in building community.

In rural areas, it may be difficult to find groups of nonbinary and transgender people. But through social media outlets such as Snapchat, Facebook, and Instagram, large groups of people are able to interact with each other. Trans and nonbinary people can ask questions about doctor visits. People can support each other in the coming out process, especially when family or friends may not initially understand. Social media also allows trans and nonbinary youth to see trans and nonbinary adults in the world. This kind of support and representation is important when face-to-face interaction is not available.

Transgender celebrities such as Jazz Jennings can be positive role models. They show trans people that they are not alone and bring visibility to issues trans people face.

gender binary, signifying an important change in how younger people see and interact with their gender. Rather than being a fixed identity given at birth, gender is a concept that can be fluid.

But as more and more people come out as nonbinary, gender nonconforming, or transgender, society must keep up. Small acts such as telling a student or adult where they are allowed to use the restroom can have a huge ripple effect. Refusing to a use a trans person's name and pronouns is linked to an increased risk of suicidal thoughts. As research has shown, instead of making a person cisgender, invalidation only serves to increase feelings of anxiety and depression.

Treatments for GD such as hormone therapy and affirming talk therapies are lifelong practices. Surgeries give people with GD the outward appearance to match their identity. But if society continues to tell trans and gender nonconforming people that they are less valued than cisgender people, gender dysphoria will continue to be an issue.

Gender variant people who suffer from dysphoria are more than their symptoms. With the help of online resources, a community of trans and gender nonconforming people have come together to share stories and support. It is this support that people with gender dysphoria say is the most helpful. Ty, a twenty-one-year-old trans man, said that watching YouTube videos of other people in transition was helpful. In an interview with the *Daily Dot*, he said, "It really helped me feel like I wasn't alone and had a lot to look forward to. I think that anyone who is struggling with dysphoria should know that they aren't alone and, if possible, find an outlet to express their feelings and role models they can look to."[43] Other trans and nonbinary people echoed Ty's sentiment.

> "I think that anyone who is struggling with dysphoria should know that they aren't alone."[43]
>
> *– Ty, a twenty-one-year-old trans man*

But it's not just about getting support from other people with gender dysphoria. The best way to support a person with gender dysphoria is to treat them like a person, and affirm their identity. Activists say people don't need to understand a person's gender identity in order to support them. People should always use a trans person's chosen name and pronoun. Friends can go shopping to help a trans person find clothes or makeup that makes them feel confident. The most important thing a community can do for a trans person is accept them for who they are.

SOURCE NOTES

INTRODUCTION: AIDEN'S STORY

1. "An Ally's Guide to Terminology," *GLAAD*, 2012. www.glaad.org.

CHAPTER 1: WHAT IS GENDER DYSPHORIA?

2. Quoted in Katy Steinmetz, "This Is What Intersex Means," *Time*, November 21, 2014. http://time.com.

3. Quoted in Vera Papisova and Evaan Kheraj, "Why Intersex Genital Mutilation Needs to Stop," *Teen Vogue*, June 29, 2017. www.teenvogue.com.

4. Quoted in Sara Reardon, "The Spectrum of Sex Development: Eric Vilain and the Intersex Controversy," *Nature*, May 10, 2016. www.nature.com.

5. Quoted in Claire Ainsworth, "Sex Redefined," *Nature*, February 18, 2015. www.nature.com.

6. Quoted in Ainsworth, "Sex Redefined."

7. Quoted in KC Clements, "What Does It Mean to Misgender Someone?" *Healthline*, October 19, 2017. www.healthline.com.

8. Clements, "What Does It Mean to Misgender Someone?"

9. Quoted in Serena Sonoma, "10 Transgender and Non-Binary People Explain What Gender Dysphoria Feels Like," *Daily Dot*, June 11, 2018. www.dailydot.com.

10. Quoted in Kristin Della Volpe, "Transgender Research: The Role of Biology in Gender Identity Development," *EndocrineWeb*, August 19, 2016. www.endocrineweb.com.

11. Quoted in Volpe, "Transgender Research."

12. Athena Edmonds, "Transgender Non-Conforming Youth: One Experience of Many," *American Psychiatric Association*, n.d. www.psychiatry.org.

13. Quoted in Anna Swartz, "LGBTQ Identity Is Shaped by Language. So What Words Will Describe 'Queer' in the Future?" *Mic*, June 18, 2018. www.mic.com.

CHAPTER 2: HOW IS GENDER DYSPHORIA DIAGNOSED?

14. *"DSM* History," *American Psychiatric Association,* n.d. www.psychiatry.org.

15. Roger K. Blashfield et al., "The Cycle of Classification: *DSM-I* Through *DSM-5*," *Annual Review of Clinical Psychology*, March 2014. www.annualreviews.org.

16. Quoted in Group for the Advancement of Psychiatry, "The History of Psychiatry & Homosexuality," *Association of Gay & Lesbian Psychiatrists*, 2012. http://aglp.org/gap.

17. Quoted in Camille Beredjick, *"DSM-V* to Rename Gender Identity Disorder 'Gender Dysphoria'," *Advocate,* July 23, 2012. www.advocate.com.

18. Quoted in Beredjick, *"DSM-V* to Rename Gender Identity Disorder 'Gender Dysphoria'."

19. Quoted in Zack Ford, "APA Issues Position Statements Supporting Transgender Care and Civil Rights," *ThinkProgress*, August 21, 2012. http://thinkprogress.org.

20. Quoted in Sarah Karlan, "We Asked People to Illustrate Their Gender Dysphoria," *BuzzFeed*, May 10, 2016. www.buzzfeed.com.

21. Quoted in Rita Braver, "Born This Way: Stories of Young Transgender Children," *CBS*, June 8, 2014. www.cbsnews.com.

22. Quoted in Daniel Trotta, "Transgender Patients Face Fear and Stigma in the Doctor's Office," *Reuters*, September 15, 2016. www.reuters.com.

23. Quoted in University of British Columbia, "Transgender Youth Avoid Health Care Due to Discomfort with Doctors," *Science Daily*, December 5, 2017. www.sciencedaily.com.

24. Quoted in University of British Columbia, "Transgender Youth Avoid Health Care Due to Discomfort with Doctors."

SOURCE NOTES
CONTINUED

CHAPTER 3: WHAT IS LIFE LIKE WITH GENDER DYSPHORIA?

25. Quoted in Karlan, "We Asked People to Illustrate Their Gender Dysphoria."

26. Quoted in Sarah Karlan, "20 Small Things to Do When Gender Dysphoria Gets You Down," *BuzzFeed*, December 6, 2015. www.buzzfeed.com.

27. Quoted in Karlan, "We Asked People to Illustrate Their Gender Dysphoria."

28. Quoted in Zing Tsjeng, "Inside the Landmark, Long Overdue Study on Chest Binding," *Vice*, September 28, 2016. www.vice.com.

29. Quoted in Tsjeng, "Inside the Landmark, Long Overdue Study on Chest Binding."

30. Quoted in Tsjeng, "Inside the Landmark, Long Overdue Study on Chest Binding."

31. Cincinnati Children's Hospital Medical Center, "High Rates of Suicide and Self-Harm Among Transgender Youth," *Science Daily*, August 31, 2016. www.sciencedaily.com.

32. Sonoma, "10 Transgender and Non-Binary People Explain What Gender Dysphoria Feels Like."

33. Quoted in Julia Glum, "Transgender Students Avoid School Bathrooms Despite Health Consequences: Report," *Newsweek*, April 12, 2017. www.newsweek.com.

34. Quoted in Adryan Corcione, "How Trauma Affects Queer and Trans Youth," *Teen Vogue*, June 29, 2018. www.teenvogue.com.

35. Quoted in Corcione, "How Trauma Affects Queer and Trans Youth."

36. Quoted in Karen Ocamb, "LGBT PTSD, the ADA and Disability Rights— Why It Matters," *Equality California*, July 22, 2016. www.eqca.org.

37. Quoted in Calla Wahlquist, "Transgender and Homeless: The Young People Who Can't Get the Support They Need," *Guardian*, April 5, 2017. www.theguardian.com.

CHAPTER 4: HOW IS GENDER DYSPHORIA TREATED?

38. Springer, "Gender-Affirming Restrooms Recommended for Schools," *Science Daily*, March 30, 2017. www.sciencedaily.com.

39. Quoted in Chris Godfrey, "What's in Choosing a Name for Trans People," *Advocate*, March 7, 2016. www.advocate.com.

40. Quoted in Godfrey, "What's in Choosing a Name for Trans People."

41. Quoted in "Mayo Provides Integrated Care for People with Gender Dysphoria," *Mayo Clinic*, August 7, 2015. www.mayoclinic.org.

42. Quoted in Christopher Wanjek, "Pausing Puberty with Hormone Blockers May Help Transgender Kids," *Live Science*, May 6, 2015. www.livescience.com.

43. Quoted in Sonoma, "10 Transgender and Non-Binary People Explain What Gender Dysphoria Feels Like."

FOR FURTHER RESEARCH

BOOKS

Archie Bongiovanni and Tristan Jimerson, *A Quick and Easy Guide to They/Them Pronouns*. Portland, OR: Limerence Press, 2018.

Maria Cook, *Gender Identity: Beyond Pronouns and Bathrooms*. White River Junction, VT: Nomad Press, 2019.

Kris Hirschmann, *Understanding Sexual Identity and Orientation*. San Diego, CA: ReferencePoint, 2018.

Ellen McGrody, *Coping with Gender Dysphoria*. New York: Rosen Publishing, 2018.

INTERNET SOURCES

APA, "What Is Gender Dysphoria?" *American Psychiatric Association*, February 2016. www.psychiatry.org.

Chris Godfrey, "What's in Choosing a Name for Trans People," *Advocate*, March 7, 2016. www.advocate.com.

Jamiles Lartey, "Risk of Poverty and Suicide Far Higher Among Transgender People, Survey Finds," *Guardian*, December 8, 2016. www.theguardian.com.

Mihran Nersesyan, "9 Keys for Dealing with Gender Dysphoria for Gender Queer & Trans Folks," *The Body Is Not an Apology*, November 15, 2017. http://thebodyisnotanapology.com.

WEBSITES

American Psychiatric Association: *Diagnostic and Statistical Manual of Mental Disorders (DSM–5)*
www.psychiatry.org/psychiatrists/practice/dsm

The American Psychiatric Association's *Diagnostic and Statistical Manual* is used by medical professionals to diagnose mental disorders.

Center of Excellence for Transgender Health
www.transhealth.ucsf.edu

The University of California, San Francisco's Center of Excellence for Transgender Health is one of the foremost trans health clinics in the United States. The center's website features a large selection of resources and research.

GLSEN
www.glsen.org

GLSEN is an organization that helps create safer schools for LGBTQ students.

Transgender Health
www.transgenderhealth.com

Transgender Health is an online collection of health resources and information for transgender people.

The Trevor Project
www.thetrevorproject.org

The Trevor Project is a suicide-prevention website for LGBTQ youth. It has a twenty-four-hour crisis hotline.

INDEX

INDEX CONTINUED

IMAGE CREDITS

ABOUT
THE AUTHOR

Martha Lundin is a genderqueer writer and educator living in Minnesota. Martha uses the gender-neutral pronouns they/them. They write books for young people full-time and teach college students part-time.